Three-Dimensional Leadership

A Balanced Approach to Leadership Success

First Printing: 2017

ISBN 978-0-578-60284-4

Chapter 1: Another Look at Leadership

After spending over 24 years in the military and more than 16
years in ordained ministry, I have determined that one word
has been constant in every circle and that word is
"leadership." From my first day meeting with an Air Force
recruiter who gave me a key chain that said, "Leadership
Excellence Starts Here" to the constant cries of senior
military and church officials begging for more leadership
from those under their charge, the desire for stronger leaders
has been the holy grail of my life. How do we get better
leaders? Are leaders born or made? What makes a good
leader? What's the difference between leaders and managers?
The list of questions about leadership goes on and on and the
number of books about leadership seems to multiply daily.
I've been introduced to concepts like situational leadership,
organizational leadership and servant leadership. I've read
books about the leadership styles of Jesus, Martin Luther
King, Jr, Attila the Hun and Abraham Lincoln. I've watched
leaders that I considered both good and bad to determine
how a person could become the best leader possible. In all
that, I've come to believe that, like doctors who practice
medicine and lawyers who practice law, those in positions of
power and influence are simply practicing leadership. They
are practicing leadership because every case seems to be

different and therefore there isn't one book answer to turn to. Leaders must do the best they can with what they have in a desire to produce the most profitable result.

It's into this conflagration of desire for better leaders and confusion on how to get them that I offer my thoughts on building better leaders. Some will want to argue with me right there because I say I am offering my thoughts on "building better leaders" because, in their opinion, leaders are born and not made. Due to my belief that leadership is about influence, I can agree that leaders can be born. After all, a person with attractive qualities like an imposing stature, powerful voice or innate physical ability will unsurprisingly draw people to themselves based on their natural-borne attractiveness. Followers will select these people as their leaders based on the gifts those individuals received from birth. This certainly indicates leaders are born. However, <u>better</u> leaders are made. If natural abilities are not enhanced, leaders relying solely on the qualities they were born with will ultimately be ineffective.

This is where three-dimensional leadership comes in. Why three-dimensional leadership? I'm glad you asked. In every situation requiring leadership, there are three elements that the leader must successfully handle in order to be a success.

The element we are most used to discussing is <u>the task</u>. If leaders don't accomplish the task at hand, they are considered failures. However, accomplishing the task is only one-third of the story. The second element that gets a lot of attention as well is <u>the team.</u> Traditionally, the people-oriented leaders will tell us the team is where all the leader's attention should be and the leader must be about taking care of his or her people. No argument here. But if the leader takes care of the people and the task remains undone, again, the leader is subpar. Conversely, even if the leader does accomplish the task but the people are run down and beat up, I would repeat that the leader is subpar. There must be a balance between leading the task and the team. But I started this section asserting that there are three elements for a leader to address. If we are working to ensure completion of the task and demonstrate support for the team, then what's left? The final element is <u>the leader.</u> This is the least mentioned part of leadership success which explains the number of leaders that burn out way before their time. A leader that does not precisely lead themselves cannot maintain the success meant for them to have. If God's plan is for a leader to lead for 30 years but, because of poor life habits, the leader does amazing things for only 10 years, that leader is subpar. The 10 years are surely something to be celebrated but it is woefully short of the goal of their Creator. The leader took care of the task and the team but, because they failed to take care of themselves, they have missed the mark and the great things that should have occurred under their guidance never happened.

Since we tend to be people of extremes, there is a desire for many of us to run for one of the three corners of the leadership triangle I have formed to make a case for that element being the most important. The "mission-first" crowd will stomp on the table and demand that all energy be focused on getting the job done. The "people-first" crowd will hold hands with those in their corner and remind everyone that without the people, the mission can never get done. Then the few people that will willingly stand in the "me-first" crowd will attest that without the leader, the people will be "like sheep without a shepherd." Everyone will run to the camp which makes them feel most comfortable. The goal of this book is to draw everyone to the middle. Our desire is for leaders to be great and, in our context, greatness in leadership means leaders who demonstrate the ability to successfully handle the task, the team and themselves. Only by effectively leading in all three areas can a leader be a true success.

Taking a 3-D Look at Yourself

1. Are you a leader? Why or why not?

2. Would you classify your leadership style as "mission-first," "people-first" or "me-first?"

3. If you were to accept the challenge of becoming a three-dimensional leader, which dimension, would you need to spend the most time working on to achieve the balance depicted in this chapter?

4. Name the leader(s) you most respect. What about them makes you want to follow them?

5. Do you believe leaders are born or made? What does your opinion mean for you as a leader?

Chapter 2: Leaders DARE the Task

Far better is it to dare mighty things, to win glorious triumphs, even though checkered by failure... than to rank with those poor spirits who neither enjoy nor suffer much, because they live in a gray twilight that knows not victory nor defeat.

-- Theodore Roosevelt

When it comes to leadership situations, many consider the most important aspect of the situation to be the task at hand. Leaders simply must get things done. We expect leaders to move things forward which highlights the generalized difference between leaders and managers. Managers are perceived to be those who are simply maintaining the status quo. If what works still works, then all is well. However, I've never heard an impassioned call across the country for managers. The hunger and thirst for change and forward motion is palpable in all areas of our society and for that change and forward motion to occur, we don't just need leaders…we need leaders who DARE.

As far as I'm concerned, "DARE" is a great word even if I wasn't using it as an acronym. The picture that always appears in my mind when I hear "DARE" is the movie, "Christmas Story." For those who have not seen the greatest

Christmas movie ever, "Christmas Story" is the first-person telling of a young boy's quest to get a Red Ryder BB gun for Christmas. During this journey for the ultimate gift, there is a scene where a young friend of the protagonist is challenged to put his tongue on a frozen pole to test the theory that a tongue will stick to a frozen pole. The immortal words that ultimately push the challenger into putting his tongue on the pole are "I triple-dog DARE you." This young man was challenged to demonstrate courage in the face of opposition and therefore I can't think of a better word for what we need from leaders today. We are desperately in need of leaders to demonstrate courage in the face of opposition or simply, to DARE. To DARE in relation to the task, leaders must DECIDE, ACT, RECOVER and ENERGIZE.

The risk of a wrong decision is preferable to the terror of indecision.
-- Maimonides

Perhaps there is nothing worse than sitting around waiting for a leader to make a decision. So often in my experience I have watched leaders "kick the can" down the road delaying a decision for an indeterminate amount of time. The wait was so agonizing that we didn't really care what the decision was, we just wanted the person in charge to pick something. This

7

experience is why the first thing I list in how leaders must DARE the task is to DECIDE. A person who is afraid to decide is afraid to lead. Given the constant questioning of every decision made, I can certainly sympathize with this fear. However, leaders must draw a line between questioning the quality of the decision versus the quality of the execution.

For example, let's say a head football coach with the best running back and offensive line in the league decides with seconds left on the clock to go for a touchdown from the one-yard line to win the game rather than kicking a field goal for the tie. As the play begins, the quarterback trips over the foot of a pulling lineman and drops the ball. The play is stopped and the team loses. At this point, armchair quarterbacks and sports pundits all over the world begin to argue about the quality of the decision with many chiming in that this was a bad decision. The rationale for saying the coach made a bad decision is that the team lost the game. But what we must ask ourselves is whether the decision, or the execution of that decision, was bad because there is a difference. We were given the fact that the coach had the best running back with the best offensive line and only needed one yard for the win. Therefore, I'd argue the odds were in the coach's favor that he would win the game. If a leader can consider all the information and determine that the probability of success is greater than the probability of failure, then the decision can be considered a good one.

Unfortunately, because hindsight is 20/20, those looking at the decision afterwards expect the coach to make a decision based off of things he didn't know would happen. If the coach knew the quarterback would drop the ball and the team would lose the game as a result and he still decided to go for the touchdown, I'd say he made a bad decision. In our example, the execution of the play was the problem and this is the issue in a lot of our leadership situations. Leaders cannot acquire all the information and must make the best decisions possible with the information they have.

I've heard others argue that the information age has slowed down the decision-making process because the massive amounts of data available seems to demand every rock be turned over before any decision is made. However, because we don't know what we don't know and most tasks have deadlines, leaders must quickly amass information, focus on what is important and then DECIDE. Leaders must also prepare for the blowback that will come if the results are contrary to what was anticipated. In the face of this criticism, leaders should always review the decision-making process but should also consider whether the problem was the decision itself, the communication of that decision or the execution.

A friend of mine in college used to constantly say, "Indecision is a decision." If leaders are going to DARE, indecision cannot be an option. Leaders must DECIDE.

Our goals can only be reached through a vehicle of a plan, in which we must fervently believe, and upon which we must vigorously act. There is no other route to success.
-- Pablo Picasso

Our friends at Alcoholics Anonymous have made it clear that the first step to recovery is admitting you have a problem. A decision must be made that something is wrong and that is indeed a huge step. However, for the step to mean something, action must follow the decision. What's true for the alcoholic trying to recover is true for the leader trying to be successful. The first step in dealing with a task is to decide and the second step is to do something about that decision. In a word, "ACT." How many times have we built beautiful plans that promise amazing results but then we put those plans on the shelf to never see the light of day? Brilliant plans never put into motion will always fail to produce anything.

There are two ways for a leader to ACT to make a task successful. Either the leader must take the first step to get the job done or the leader must remove any barriers from in front of the team so the team members can get the job done. The thought of the leader taking the first step is very popular with many people because it pictures the leader "getting her hands dirty." This evokes the statement I've heard from many leaders before, "I won't ask you to do anything that I won't do myself." Admittedly I've been in positions where those words were just lip service. However, the leader took on a whole new image in my mind when she rolled up her sleeves and began to move the task towards completion. A leader who chooses to ACT personally after making the decision, especially when the task is formidable, will inspire the members to follow and give the actions of the team a greater chance at success.

The counter to the leader being the first to ACT is the cliché, "If you want something done right, you need to do it yourself." This has been the death of many leaders as they've attempted to do all the work themselves for fear the team wouldn't complete the task the "right" way. If leaders are tempted to respond to tasks in this way, then their first ACT must be to remove themselves so the team can do what the team does best. This is where delegation comes in. When I took my last CPR class, we were taught to first assess the scene before rendering aid. We had to DECIDE if it was safe. Once we determined it was safe, we had to ACT and this ACT took on two forms. First, we had to render whatever aid was necessary. Second, we had to request assistance from any bystanders. The instructor informed us that it wasn't enough for us to yell out, "Call 9-1-1." Due to human nature, people hearing that directive instinctively assume someone else is going to make the call resulting in nobody making the call. We were told to point at a person and direct that person to make the call. Leaders must do the same thing. For a leader to sit in a meeting and say, "OK team here's what we're going to do" but not assign anyone to accomplish the task is a failure to ACT. Everyone leaves the meeting celebrating the marvelous idea just presented but nobody moves forward to implement the decision. This is how we too often fail a task before we even get started. We simply do not ACT. If a leader is going to DARE, the process cannot stop with the decision. The leader must ACT by taking the first step towards task completion or directing others to begin the work.

Mistakes are part of the game. It's how well you recover from them, that's the mark of a great player.
-- Alice Cooper

Attitude reflects leadership. When things don't go right, everyone will look to the leader for direction in how to respond. If the leader spends two weeks fretting about the previous failure, that leader can expect the team to take at least another week to return to form. Leaders must RECOVER quickly from tasks that don't go well so they can rapidly lead the team to success in the next task.

Using an analogy from the world of football, New York Giants' quarterback Eli Manning took a lot of criticism early in his career because of the way he responded to setbacks. After a negative play, NFL cameramen would zoom in on Eli's face to see his reaction and one of the announcers would quickly say, "He can't act like that because the rest of the team is watching him." I don't know whether they knew it or not but the announcers were discussing the essence of the requirement for leaders to RECOVER. Eli is the leader of the Giants' offense so when things go wrong, the team looks to him for their visual cues on how they are to respond. If they get back in the huddle and Eli is still complaining about the previous play, the rest of the team is going to continue to complain about the previous play. With all the complaining about the previous play, nobody is paying attention to what's supposed to happen on the next play and if the next play has negative results as well, the spiral to defeat has begun.

Every time something bad happened to me while I was growing up my dad would utter the two words that became the bane of my existence, "builds character." His point was that the things I was suffering from were going to serve to build greater character in me for the future. I hated to hear those words because they simply said to me that I had to "suck it up" and move on which is exactly what I didn't want to do. I wanted to wallow in the misery of my situation. However, my father wanted me to look beyond the current situation and prepare for whatever was to come. He was convinced that my current situation couldn't stop me from future success and could be used to improve the probability of that success. While I could engage in a profound argument about whether difficult times build or display character, there is no argument that my father was telling me to RECOVER.

Things will go wrong. The greatest plans can quickly unravel in the face of reality and while we expect things to work for the best, we must be prepared in case things happen for the worst. To RECOVER as a leader is to ensure the task doesn't go from bad to worse and the team can put the negative event behind them and move forward towards success. However, this all depends on the leader. For every decision and every action, Murphy's Law is there, and the

14

only way to beat Murphy is to not admire the failures but to RECOVER and move toward the future.

Enthusiasm is the yeast that makes your hopes shine to the stars. Enthusiasm is the sparkle in your eyes, the swing in your gait. The grip of your hand, the irresistible surge of will and energy to execute your ideas.
-- Henry Ford

After winning the Super Bowl in 2016, Denver Broncos' General Manager John Elway talked about why he decided to let former head coach John Fox go before the end of his contract. By all accounts Coach Fox had been a successful leader. In his three years as head coach, the Broncos had the conference's best record each year and played in a Super Bowl. Other coaches and teams would kill for this level of success. However, it wasn't enough for John Elway. He cited the fact that even though they had the best record and home field advantage two of those years, the Broncos lost in the first round of the playoffs because, in his opinion, Coach Fox didn't get the team excited to play. In Mr. Elway's opinion, and in my terminology, Coach Fox failed to ENERGIZE the task. He didn't do enough to get the team excited about the task at hand and that lack of energy resulted in defeat.

The irony of that example is that most of us armchair quarterbacks (and coaches) will ask "how hard is it to get players excited to play in a playoff game or the Super Bowl. You should have to just point and tell them to do their jobs. Sounds great, but Coach Fox faced the same dilemma as the shift manager at McDonald's. Yes, the task ahead is the person's job and they are being paid to complete that job and their performance will determine whether they keep that job. Those three facts are enough for many people to get to work. Unfortunately, those criteria don't work on everyone. Some will say, "I don't care if it's my job, I don't want to do it." Others will add, "The money's not that great anyways." The last group will tell us, "Please fire me because there has to be something better out there." We could go on and, if you've ever led, you could probably share some other statements you've heard when presenting someone with the task. And this element of bringing energy to the task is what sets better leaders apart. The leader must find a way to ENERGIZE the same task for different members of the team.

Because I tend to be a Type-A, get-the-job-done type of guy, I expect everyone else to be the same. Give me a task and I'm going to do it because it's my job. It was an absolute shock to me that there were people out there who asked one very simple question, "Why should I?" I explained the points

I made above but to no avail. I could write them a bad report or give them a letter of counseling but all that did was distract all of us from getting the task completed. I had to learn what motivated that person and apply what I learned to the situation so the person would run headlong into the task to achieve success. This reminds of the preacher who said, "I don't love all my kids the same. I love all my kids differently…because they are all different." This should be the motto of every leader hoping to ENERGIZE a task. We must lead everyone differently because they are all different. Some are purely motivated by the challenge and we must amplify the challenge to ENERGIZE the task for them. Others are motivated by knowing the big picture of the task so we must bring that out to ENERGIZE the task for them. Still others are motivated by what's in it for them so we must let them know the personal impact to ENERGIZE the task for that group. While we might not agree with the motivations of those on the team, they are all the team members we have so we need to learn how to lead them. The goal is to get the task done and if the leader doesn't ENERGIZE the most mundane task, some success is possible but the true success we're looking for won't happen. Just ask John Fox.

Taking a 3-D Look at Yourself

1. What is your process for making decisions?

2. What decision have you made that you have delayed to ACT on? What are you waiting for?

3. How do you respond to adversity? What would those you lead say about how you handle adversity?

4. Consider the person who is your toughest leadership challenge. What would it take to ENERGIZE that person to improve their work performance?

Chapter 3: Leaders CARE for the Team

Nobody cares how much you know, until they know how much you care.

-- Theodore Roosevelt

My pastor in North Carolina made a point to say "Nobody gets to pick their boss but everyone picks their leader." When she first uttered those words I didn't understand but, as I mulled her words over, they made great sense. The selection of the boss is initiated from the top down. Presidents pick Vice Presidents who pick directors who pick managers who pick supervisors and so on. Those are the people placed in charge but they are not necessarily the leaders. Oh, they have the titles, the expense accounts and the corner offices but they aren't the leader unless someone chooses to follow them. I learned this lesson first hand when I took command of the Air Force ROTC detachment at North Carolina A&T State University. When I arrived on campus I was the highest-ranking Air Force officer in Greensboro, NC. I had the title: Commander and Professor of Aerospace Studies. I had the pin on my uniform and the orders in my hand that both testified that I was the commander. I even had the biggest office. It didn't take long for me to notice that those things certainly made me the boss but I had a long way to go before I was the leader. The cadets knew that due to my rank, my pin, my orders and my title that the Air Force made me the boss. However, they had chosen another leader. Whenever I'd have all the cadets together and I would bark some orders, I noticed the cadets would look over at the Major who worked for me to see her reaction. If she nodded, the cadets would gladly move in the direction of my orders. At first, I was offended because I had everything necessary to be in charge but they still ran to her for direction. The truth is I had everything but them. They didn't know me so my experience, rank and other attributes meant nothing because there was no relationship. In nearly every survey I've ever seen about what followers want in their leaders, the number one trait they desire is that their leaders CARE.

The concept of caring about the people gives many a view of a touchy-feely group that is more concerned about the temperature of the bottled water in the fridge than getting the work done. However, great leaders understand that if they take care of the people, the people will take care of the mission. I've worked for some bosses that were incredibly smart but didn't have any people skills whatsoever. I will not call them my leader because I wasn't following them. I was doing what those bosses told me because it was the right thing to do but I would consider any success we had occurred despite them and not because of them. Those bosses didn't CARE about me so I did my job and left it at that. On the other hand, there are those that I would run through a wall for right now if they called me. They didn't have all the accolades of the other bosses but I knew they cared and that inspired me to go further than I ever thought possible in order to please them and make them look good. What ultimately mattered was how those I chose to be my leader related to me. Somehow, I doubt I'm the only one who is looking for that kind of leader. In addition to attacking a task with DARE, successful leaders must handle the team with CARE. For our purposes, to CARE is to COVER, AFFIRM, RESPECT and EMPOWER.

Yea, though I walk through the valley of the shadow of death, I will fear no evil; For You are with me; Your rod and Your staff, they comfort me.
-- Psalm 23:4

When I was younger I used to wear a t-shirt with the phrase "God's got my back" emblazoned on the back. The words on the shirt served to inspire confidence that no matter what I faced, God was with me. That didn't mean He was happy with everything I was doing but it did mean that I could count on Him to protect me when times got tough. In a word, God, as my leader, was giving me COVER. Unfortunately, the concept of leaders providing COVER for members of the team carries negative connotations. I am not suggesting in the slightest that leaders cover up illegal or incorrect things done by followers. It is a poor leader who refuses to discipline followers or ignores illegal or immoral activities. In the end, that type of leader isn't covering their followers but covering themselves in an attempt to make things look better than they really are. What I mean by COVER is that the followers know the leader will be there to assist and protect the follower in every situation.

Due to the prevailing "take care of number one" attitude in the world today, this concept is foreign to many people. When bad things start to happen, everyone cuts and runs to leave the slowest to move holding the bag and taking the blame. Many of us have been in situations where, when results were less-than-expected, the "leader" disavowed any knowledge of the events in order to place blame somewhere else. What a refreshing world this would be if leaders lived in accordance with the old adage and "went down with the ship."

The best example of this was once when I was asked to preach by a friend of mine. As a part of the conversation he casually uttered the phrase, "I beat my sheep." What he was subtly telling me was that if there was any discipline or harsh words to be handed out to his congregation, he would be the one to hand it out. Those were his people and nobody else was going to come in and abuse them. He had them covered. I always saw my job as a supervisor while on active duty to keep the higher ups off the backs of my people so they were free to do their jobs. I believed if I provided the COVER they needed, they would do great things.

Stop being a critic and be a light; don't be a judge, be a model. I think we are far too critical. I think the best way to correct behavior is to accentuate and affirm positive behavior and to ignore negative behavior. Generally speaking, there is a time to correct, of course; but my biggest advice would be, 'Affirm your child.'
-- Sean Covey

My parents were polar opposites when it came to addressing the things I was doing. My dad was a perfectionist. If I played baseball and hit safely in 49 out of 50 at-bats, we were sure to discuss, at great length mind you, that 50th at-bat. There was always room for improvement and he believed there was learning in those failures and we needed to mine them for all they were worth. My mom on the other hand was the ultimate encourager. If, instead of hitting safely in those 49 out of 50 at- bats, I struck out 50 times, my mom would tell me how beautiful my swing was. She was going to find something to praise no matter how small it was or how silly anyone else thought she was being. My mom's focus was to AFFIRM me in the midst of every situation. Now I will admit that too much of either of these would have ruined my potential for success. Too much focusing on the failures would have made me feel like I was never good enough. Too much celebration of "my good swing" would have left me satisfied with just swinging and never hitting anything. My parents struck a tremendous balance and successful leaders must strike a similar balance to ensure the growth of the team. Many of us are extremely good at pointing out the faults of those who work for us. We've convinced ourselves that we're just trying to make them better and pointing out their mistakes is the best way to do that. However, because we expect people to do their jobs, we ignore the other side of the scale and never AFFIRM those around us. This typically results in team members who feel underappreciated by management and dissatisfied with the work environment. After all, if the boss doesn't appreciate what I'm doing, why should I do it? That last line is a smack in the face of many Type A personalities because we would respond, "You should do it because it's your job." And that is true but there are personality types out there who like to know that someone in authority recognizes their hard work. Just because we as leaders don't need to have anyone AFFIRM us doesn't mean those who work for us don't.

We see this lack of balance when we're called to the leader's office. Even at the end of my 24-year Air Force career, whenever my boss called me and requested I come to his office, I felt a lump in my throat and something in the pit of my stomach. I had no idea why he wanted to see me, but my assumption was that whatever the reason, it was bad. Could it be that the only time he ever asked me to come to his office was to berate me for some failure? My response was learned over time because words of affirmation from leadership were few and far between. Therefore, when someone in authority spoke, the general expectation was that bad news was coming. Successful leaders cannot fall into this trap because they will lose the hearts and minds of the people they need to complete the tasks at hand.

I feel I must continue to stress this isn't about whitewashing failures. Poor performance must be addressed and corrected. However, leaders should interact with their team members more than in just a corrective mode. When I was the Commander of Air Force ROTC Detachment 605 at North

Carolina A&T State University, in order to eliminate the fear of coming to the boss' office, I made it a habit to specifically call students to my office to tell them something good I had seen and to see how they were doing. At first it was hilarious to watch them slowly approach my office with fear and trepidation on their faces expecting me to drop the hammer. To see their faces, light up when I told them about how good their uniform looked or how I appreciated the work they did helping another cadet was worth the extra time it took. The time I took to AFFIRM their work paid huge dividends in the end because they knew I was watching not just to catch them doing wrong but to see them doing right. Another thing I did was to thank my team members at the end of every work day. Why should I do this because they were doing their jobs? I did it for exactly that reason. They were doing their jobs which we tend to take for granted. They very well could have called in sick that day. They could have taken shortcuts all day long and left work for someone else to do. But they didn't and I wanted to let them know that I appreciated their efforts. I admit I've taken a lot of grief for this desire to regularly and consistently AFFIRM my team members. However, I do believe my words of AFFIRMATION to those who have worked with for me spurred a desire for them to work harder on the task because they knew I appreciated their efforts.

I'm not concerned with your liking or disliking me... All I ask is that you respect me as a human being.
-- Jackie Robinson

When Aretha Franklin released "Respect" in April 1967 I can't believe there was any doubt that the song would be an instant hit. Why? Because people then, and certainly now, are clamoring for the respect of those around them. Therefore, it should be no surprise when I say leaders must RESPECT the members of the team to be successful. Nobody wants to work for a boss that doesn't RESPECT them. There is something deep inside every individual that craves to be "held in esteem or honor" which is the dictionary.com definition for RESPECT (Dictionary.com, accessed 17 May 16). Unfortunately, this is where most of us stop. We understand the definition of the word and we know to say we RESPECT those we work with but the elephant in the room for every successful leader is "what does RESPECT look like?" How does someone know you RESPECT them?

Gary Chapman is the author of the best-selling book, "The 5 Love Languages." In the book, he details that love looks different to different people. Therefore, if someone is to know that you love them, you need to speak their love language. I believe there is a parallel to RESPECT. What

RESPECT looks like to one person may not be the same way that RESPECT looks to another. Therefore, to truly RESPECT the persons on the team, the leader must get to know them and determine what they value and then demonstrate RESPECT for what that individual values. One of the places where I see this thought abused the most is in regard to time. The meeting is supposed to start at one but only half the team is there. Instead of starting the meeting at one, the leader decides to give the rest of the team a little more time which usually equates to 10 or 15 minutes. Once "enough" people show up, the meeting begins and the leader feels successful because she got the majority of the people there and passed out the necessary information. What she missed is the fact that she failed to RESPECT the time of those who made the effort to be on time. But Bob you say, "I don't want to have to repeat myself so I wait for others to show up." Even in that statement we should hear our own selfishness. We feel it's OK to "waste" the time of those who showed up on time so we don't have to "waste" our time repeating ourselves later. In my humble opinion, that is the epitome of a leader who lacks RESPECT for those on the team. Everyone is busy. Everyone's time matters. However, successful leaders will take the hit so team members can move forward.

When I was a young Air Force officer it always amazed me when senior leaders would come in trumpeting some great idea they thought would be fun for us. This great idea was formulated by a bunch of 40-something officers working hard to define fun for a bunch of 20-something officers. As you might guess, the definitions were vastly different. What was even scarier was when I became the 40-something officer and started devising fun for those 20-somethings that worked for me. At the end of one of those meetings something hit me and I determined, "I have become them." What my peers and the leaders before me failed to do during our strategy sessions was to walk a mile in the shoes of those who came behind us. To a person we would readily admit that we hated it when our superiors devised fun for us but when we got to the leadership position, we did what was done before us. We forgot what it was like and that shows a lack of RESPECT for the plight of those we lead. This doesn't mean we will always do what makes folks happy. That's impossible when leaders must balance mission requirements and personnel needs. What it does mean is successful leaders will at least consider the needs of team members as part of the decisions that need to be made.

One final thought about RESPECT. We've heard it said perhaps dozens of times that a good leader doesn't ask the team members to do anything they wouldn't do. I think this is important to not just show RESPECT for the situation of the team but it can also provide first-hand knowledge to the leader on exactly how the tasks are done. The reality show, "Undercover Boss," hits on this notion by taking the owners of major corporations and putting them at the lowest levels of the business to find out exactly what their employees do on a daily basis to propel the company forward. At the end of the show, the bosses always emerge to highlight severe inefficiencies in their business practices and discover a newfound RESPECT for the people under their charge. I'm sure they respected the men and women of the company before their experience but the time spent walking in the shoes of their team opened a new world to them and ultimately made the team better. For a leader to be successful, RESPECT needs to be more than a hit song by Aretha Franklin. RESPECT needs to be an operating principle showing just how much CARE the leader has.

As we look ahead into the next century, leaders will be those who empower others.

-- Bill Gates

In the Old Testament book of Exodus there is a story about Moses leading the children of Israel out of Egypt on their way to the Promised Land. Moses' father-in-law, Jethro, shows up to see how Moses and the family are doing. While Jethro watches, Moses sits down on the judge's seat and begins to handle all the disputes the people have. This process lasted from morning till evening. At the end of the day Jethro speaks up and simply says, "What you are doing is not good" (Exodus 18:17). Actually, before making his judgement on the situation, Jethro asks a question to Moses that should be asked to leaders everywhere, "Why are you sitting by yourself, and all the people stand around you from morning to evening" (Exodus 18:14b, NET). The Bob Payne Paraphrase says, "Why are you doing this alone when there are so many other people around?" Jethro goes on to give his son-in-law some great advice about how to EMPOWER people to share the load so the team can move forward.

To EMPOWER team members is a scary proposition for many leaders because it takes control out of the leader's hands and puts it in the hands of others that may be less experienced. Many leaders have subscribed to the notion, like Moses in the example above, that if you want anything done right; you have to do it yourself. The arrogance of that statement is that the leader's way is the ONLY way to complete the task and therefore is the right way. I wish I remembered the name of the leader who taught me the meaning of EMPOWER. However, while the name has long since left me, the lesson has stuck with me for years. In my early days of the Air Force, my commander called me into his office to give me a task. He bluntly told me what he wanted done and then stopped there. I know he could see the questions on my face as I waited for him to tell me how to complete the task. The silence was deafening until he looked over at me and said (what have become immortal words in my life), "I'm not going to tell you how to suck the egg. I just want the egg sucked." Yep, it's crude and to many it might not make sense but he was telling me that his concern was that the task was completed at the right time but the "right" way was up to me. He EMPOWERED me to solve the problem on my own. It was the first time an officer had given me a task without giving me step-by-step instructions on exactly how the task was supposed to be done. It was an exhilarating experience. I left his office with a task that I could apply my thoughts and ideas to solving. I was free to create and innovate. I could problem solve without man-made boundaries. Needless to say, I was hooked on this leader and determined to follow him wherever he decided to go. I wanted to follow him because he allowed me to be a larger part of the team. No longer was I just some guy. I was a guy who had thoughts and ideas and had the authority to use those thoughts and ideas to complete the team's tasks.

Like every other aspect in the CARE section, a leader must know the team members to EMPOWER effectively. To provide decision authority to someone who isn't ready is to invite disaster. It's like giving the keys to the Ferrari to the 12-year old just because they seem like they're ready for the responsibility. The leader needs to analyze the members of the team and determine how much freedom they can handle and then EMPOWER them to operate within that sphere. As they are given opportunities to test their own meddle in making decisions and applying their own skills, they will begin to grow and be ready for additional responsibility. I heard one leader say, "The job of the leader is to work himself out of a job." The idea was simple. Leaders build leaders but to eventually be leaders, the followers must be EMPOWERED to make decisions so they can grow in their skills and abilities. A leader who CAREs, cares enough to EMPOWER his or her people so those people can grow to be leaders themselves one day.

Taking a 3-D Look at Yourself

1. Think about the way you have spoken to those you lead in the last week. Have you said anything that would make them think you CARE? If yes, what did you say? If not, why not?

2. Do you have to be a "touchy-feely people person" to CARE? If yes, what does that mean for those who don't fall into the "touchy-feely people-person category?

Chapter 4: Leaders PREPARE Themselves

By failing to prepare, you are preparing to fail.

-- Benjamin Franklin

Throughout my Air Force career, I was given a lot of credit for taking care of my people and I took tremendous pride in that. The pride only increased when I look back to see what we were able to accomplish as a team. On those two levels, I'd consider myself a success. However, I have to confess that it is this third leg of the leadership triangle that I failed at the most and, unless I'm grossly mistaken, I'm not alone. The glory of successfully accomplishing a task and the satisfaction of taking care of the team tend to greatly overshadow the leader's dedication to taking care of themselves. However, it is clear that if leaders do not PREPARE themselves, their time and effectiveness as leaders will be greatly shortened.

One of the bad things about talking about leaders preparing themselves is the visions of self-serving leaders that we have all had the unfortunate pleasure to deal with. Those folks who constantly "looked out for number one" and ultimately made everyone else "feel like number two." While I assert that leaders must look out for themselves, the purpose of looking out for themselves is not for themselves. The end of looking out for themselves is for the betterment of the team and the completion of the task. To be a true leadership success, a leader must not just DARE the task and CARE for the team, but the leader must PREPARE themselves. To PREPARE themselves for leadership success, leaders must PRIORITIZE, REST, EAT, PRAY, ASK, READ and EXERCISE.

> *To succeed today, you have to set priorities, decide what you stand for.*
> *-- Lee Iacocca*

In one of my favorite movies, "The Incredibles," part of the villain's plan was to make everyone super because "if everyone is super, then no one is." Well, what was true about superpowers in the movie is true about priorities in the real world. If everything is important, then nothing is important. Therefore, if a leader is going to lead effectively, they first need to PRIORITIZE.

Some would argue that PRIORITIZE shouldn't be something the leader does for themselves but should be done for the task. The leader must tell the team what is and what is not important. I agree with that which is why I would place that piece of prioritization under the "DECIDE" heading we discussed earlier. The leader decides what's important and communicates that decision to the team. However, if the only prioritization the leader does is in regard to the tasks, then the leader's personal life is going to suffer which will eventually detract from the leader's longevity in the position. A leader must know what's important to them. I call this knowing their own definition of success. It is easier to lead when you know what's important to you.

As I moved up in the ranks during my Air Force career and began to take on more responsibility, I forced myself to sit down and map out what my definition of success was. One very important part of my definition of success was that when I retired, I wanted the same woman I started my career with sitting in the front row at my retirement ceremony. My marriage was a priority and therefore, when I made decisions about my career, I always considered the impact my actions would have on my family. In fact, when I took over as the commander of Air Force ROTC Detachment 605, I provided my team with the following priority list so they would understand who I was:

1.   I am a person therefore I have a relationship with God

2.7   I am a partner therefore I have a relationship with my wife.

2.7 I am a parent therefore I have a relationship with my children.

2.7 I am a pastor therefore I have a relationship with my church.

2.7 I am a pal therefore I have a relationship with my friends.

2.7 I am a patriot therefore I have a relationship with my country.

2.7 I am personnel therefore I have a relationship with my job.

The reason for the unique numbering system is that for me, priority number one is ALWAYS pleasing God. I have refused to do anything that would jeopardize that relationship. Now the remaining six priorities had a little bit of flexibility to them. There were times that I had to put the needs of my wife on hold so I could satisfy a responsibility to my duties with the Air Force or the church and vice versa. It wasn't always easy to balance each of these responsibilities but this list provided a framework for me to make the decisions I needed to make.

Nobody can effectively set the priorities for another person. However, if a leader doesn't set their own priorities, someone else will gladly set priorities for them. Therefore, unless a leader wants to live out someone else's definition of success they need to PRIORITIZE for themselves.

The body needs its rest, and sleep is extremely important in any health regimen. There should be three main things: eating, exercise and sleep. All three together in the right balance make for a truly healthy lifestyle.
-- *Rohit Shetty*

I heard an amazing analogy the other day that makes the point of REST very clearly. Every person with a cell phone makes it a habit to monitor the percentage of battery left on the phone. As the number slowly decreases we make calculated decisions to determine how we make use of the remaining power. If we were to get down to around 10%, we'd be searching everywhere for an outlet because we understand the battery life on our phone is limited and, if the phone is going to be productive, it needs to be recharged. It's funny that while we recognize the limitations on our phones, we refuse to recognize the same limitations in our bodies. Leaders need to REST if they are going to be successful.

Of all the areas to PREPARE, I'd argue this is the one I've failed at the most. Despite cell phones, microwaves, iPads, cars and so many other devices designed to make our lives more efficient, we seem to be busier than ever and that busyness means there's no time to REST. However, lacking rest will eventually catch up to us as our decisions become less and less productive. Dr. Charles Stanley, pastor of First Baptist Church in Atlanta says, "Never make any decision when you are too Hungry, Angry, Lonely or Tired." I'm sure we could all sit around and detail some of the lousy decisions we made in the midst of one of these extreme emotions. Perhaps the worst decisions come when we are too tired. Study after study details how our brains border on operating like we're drunk when we don't get proper rest. No wonder that after an extended period of time without sleep, the decisions of a leader get worse and worse.

Perhaps the reason so many leaders fail at getting the REST they need is because they fail to EMPOWER their people. The mantra of the unrested leader is, "I have to be there. They can't do it without me." It is an extremely poor leader who has to be present whenever any work is being done. The bible says the pastor's job is to prepare those under their charge for the work of ministry (Ephesians 4:12). The pastor isn't supposed to be doing all the work. The pastor is supposed to prepare others to do the work. Many of us have woefully missed this and have not just burned the candle at both ends but we flat threw the candle into the fire and then wondered why we couldn't think clearly or felt run down all the time. Proper time and personnel management will afford leaders the opportunity to REST and recharge themselves. A leader can go without REST but their effectiveness will be cut short as their body seeks out what it craves so badly. I fell asleep at the wheel of my car once because while I was driving home my body decided it was going to get the sleep I had been denying it because I as "too busy to sleep." My busyness almost cost me and two others their lives in a head-on collision which I can firmly blame on being a leader who refused to get REST. Not making time for REST almost killed me and it is killing the careers of many would-be successful leaders.

It is never too late to change the way you eat - once you do, your body will thank you with a longer and healthier life.
-- David H. Murdock

Over the years it has become clear to me that most people in leadership positions are bad time managers. OK, let me take that back because I don't want to offend anyone. In my years of leadership, it has become clear to me that I am a bad time manager. How do I know? Because I constantly hear people, I mean myself, complaining that there isn't enough time. There's not enough time to get the task done. There's not enough time to do the paperwork. There's not enough time to take care of the family. There's not enough time to rest. Actually, I could have used that same line to run down every item in this chapter. We as leaders complain about the limited time available to do what needs to be done so we usually end up pushing the important away so we can accomplish the immediate. The immediate is loud. The immediate is what everyone else cares about. The immediate must be done now because someone stamped "Urgent" or "Hot" on it. Forget everything else and get the immediate done now. Unfortunately, since everybody thinks their immediate issue is the most critical thing for us and we have done nothing to PRIORITIZE our lives, the important things of life go by the wayside to our detriment. One of the important things that successful leaders have to learn to work into their schedule is making time to EAT.

I'm sure someone thinks I have gone off the deep end on this one especially if they follow me during my day. As I said when I started this, we are all "practicing leadership" and I certainly haven't arrived yet. If food is indeed the fuel our bodies need to run efficiently so we have the energy to accomplish all that is in front of us, then we must make time to EAT. Some of us have learned the hard way about this fueling issue. Then again, maybe it's just me. I remember one time when I was living in Montana. I was the chief of a section in the Operations Group with 12 people working for me and an important mission to keep moving. I was also the pastor of Union Bethel AME Church in the process of trying to grow the congregation. To say I was busy was an understatement. I would work a full day and then jump in my truck, get to the house, do a Superman change, get back in the truck and drive to the church to accomplish whatever tasks were necessary there. There were home visits and hospital visits. I was a full-sized version of the Energizer® Bunny and I kept going and going and going. I had to take care of all the immediate things and I did…until an important thing popped up. One day as I was driving home to make one of my patented Superman changes, my truck ran out of gas. Here I was trying to accomplish immediate business for God and country and I was stuck on the side of the road because I had failed to take care of something important. I hadn't fueled my vehicle. The excuses of "I just didn't have time" seemed silly at that point because I certainly didn't have time to be sitting on the side of the road waiting for someone to come help me. What was true with my truck is true in the lives of many of us. We can go quite a while without taking time to EAT but there's going to come a point where our bodies are going to break down because they don't have the fuel they need to carry out the tasks at hand. Just like my truck was useless to me sitting on the side of the road, a leader who is physically laid up on the side of the road is useless to the team and detrimental to the task.

That we need to EAT is obvious. All the studies tell us how important it is to EAT. I'm not breaking any new ground here. What I am trying to do is emphasize the importance of **making** time to EAT. Just like the principle of REST, leaders must be diligent about carving out time in their schedule to EAT. Anyone who has been a leader for long knows life isn't like elementary school when a bell would ring and everything else would stop so you can enjoy lunch. Planning to EAT must be a conscious decision. Otherwise, we will do our best to exist on potato chips and soda because "that's all we have time for." Don't worry, if that's all you have time for, when your body shuts down and you end up in the hospital, you'll have plenty of time to EAT.

I know that when I pray, something wonderful happens. Not just to the person or persons for whom I'm praying, but also something wonderful happens to me. I'm grateful that I'm heard.
-- Maya Angelou

When I give this presentation at universities I step very carefully here to not offend others with my views. In fact, I wrestled with putting PRAY into this list for fear the mention of a spiritual aspect to leadership would distract from the point I was trying to make. However, as part of being a 3-dimensional leader, I had to recognize the fact that each of us is a 3-dimensional being. Every human being is mind, body and spirit. Some would render this soul, body and spirit so if that suits you fine. The mind, or soul, is the seat of our thoughts and emotions. It is the essence of our personality. Like a three-legged stool, our lives depend on the proper balance of all three areas if we are to be effective. As you will read in this chapter, there is a lot of attention paid to the leader taking care of his or her body. In this section, you will read about why it is important to REST, EAT and EXERCISE. REST is also important for the mind/soul as is the call to PRIORITIZE, READ and ASK. That's two-thirds of the three-legged stool taken care of. However, I'd argue many of our stools are tipped over because we ignore the third part, the spiritual part, of who we are. That is why I say it is important to PRAY.

Now of course I'm a pastor of a Christian church so I attack this from a Christian frame of reference. To PRAY is to have a conversation with God. To PRAY is to share our concerns with the Creator of the universe and receive guidance from Him. I just got too mystical for some of you which will cause you to discount everything else I've said because you believe I'm some kind of quack for talking to someone who isn't there and then expecting a response. I find that funny because in a real sense I'm writing this to you and I don't know if you're there. I take it on faith that you're going to read this and respond. Similarly, I take it on faith that God exists and He cares about me and wants to hear what I have to say. And yes, I do believe He speaks back. Maybe not audibly, but the truth is you don't always respond to those who talk to you audibly. There are a myriad of ways God speaks, such as through that quiet voice in our spirit, through the bible, through other people and through our circumstances. As we pray in faith and ask for guidance and then look for God to answer in His way, and not our way, we will receive the direction we need.

Funny enough, the reason PRAY is on this list isn't because I think it's just an important spiritual discipline. PRAY is on this list because it's important for leaders to understand that the task before them is too big for them to handle alone. When any member of the armed services or political office takes the oath of office, the last four words spoken are "So help me God." I think that is incredibly significant because after professing a willingness to support and defend the Constitution and obey the orders of the officers appointed over them and to well and faithfully discharge the duties they will be assigned; every person admits the need for help from a higher power. To do all the things contained in the oath, those reciting the words are going to need help. A leader who thinks he or she has it all figured out and doesn't need help is destined to fail. To PRAY is to humble yourself and admit that you don't have all the answers and are looking for guidance to solve problems for which there aren't pat, book answers. When Solomon was elevated to be the king of Israel, God came to him in a vision and gave him a blank check to ask for anything he wanted. Solomon's response was, "Therefore give to Your servant an understanding heart to judge Your people, that I may discern between good and evil. For who is able to judge this great people of Yours?" (1 Kings 3:9) Bottom line is that Solomon chose to PRAY for wisdom so he could be a successful leader. Solomon set the pace. To PREPARE himself to lead, he chose to PRAY. Should we do anything less?

In terms of asking questions, I plead guilty. I ask a hell of a lot of questions. That's my job.
-- Dick Cheney

I remember coming home from school with homework and laying it out on the table waiting for my mother to get home. When she got home I bombarded her with questions about how to do the work. Maybe a bit overwhelmed with my aggression and the subject matter, my mom responded, "Did you ASK the teacher?" I looked at her like she was crazy and said, "No. If I asked her then she would think I didn't know what I was doing." To which my mom correctly pointed out, "Well when you take the test and get all the answers wrong, she will know you didn't know." I didn't want to ASK the teacher because I saw it as a sign of weakness and I didn't believe for whatever reason that she had my best intentions at heart. My failure to ASK endangered my ability in the class. In like manner, a leader's failure to ASK endangers her ability to lead effectively.

We all have questions and that's not a bad thing. To not have questions is to have perfect knowledge and I'm guessing there aren't too many of us that will claim that. (There was this one guy I worked with in Montana...) Similar to my call to PRAY, to ASK is to show humility in the sense that we don't have all the answers. However, instead of asking God, this ASK is to those who work above us, with us AND for us. I stress the "for us" because many leaders are too proud to ASK those in the trenches any questions for fear of being seen as unknowing. Like my mom said, when we make decisions as leaders that go against what's actually going on with the organization, everyone will know for sure we don't know what's going on. Before attacking any major task with my team, I would gather everyone together and ASK for input on how we should handle the situation. What I learned though is that the asking needed to start with the youngest and newest on the team. The youngest and newest members are often reluctant to speak when a leader poses a general question. They choose to bide their time and "pay their dues" deferring to those who have been around longer. This often results in answers being shades of "what we've always done before." Therefore, I would specifically point to those young and new members of the team and say to them, "What do you think we should do?" After the initial shock of being asked, they would eventually give an answer. This approach did two things. First, it made sure they were included and allowed their voices to be heard. Second, it forced the more experienced/older team members to come up with better ideas. My choice to ASK every member on the team gave the team a better chance at success because we were open to more possible solutions.

Anyone who knows me knows I'm not the sharpest tool in the drawer. Better yet, I know that, and while it took me time to move pass the pride of not wanting to reveal that fact, I've come to accept it and I think I've benefitted from it. I know every great and wonderful idea will not, and does not have to, come from the place where I'm standing. If I ASK, I can learn better ways of doing things and gain insight into how others see the landscape before us. Another side benefit of asking is that when someone gives a good answer, then I can EMPOWER them to put that answer into effect. This once again makes them part of the process and frees me as the leader to focus on other issues. The person has ownership of the solution because it was their idea and that ownership will most likely conclude with a better result on the task. But none of this would have been possible if I didn't ASK.

The more that you read, the more things you will know. The more that you learn, the more places you'll go.
-- Dr. Seuss

Thus far in this chapter I have challenged you to PRAY, which is to seek solutions from God. I have challenged you to ASK, which is to seek solutions from those around you. Now we move to expanding the ASK circle with the challenge to READ. To READ is to garner knowledge and perspective from those far from you in order to apply it to your current situation. To READ is to seek solutions from the world. To READ is also to exercise our minds and to challenge our views of the world. To READ is to open ourselves up to wisdom beyond the reaches of our current experience. While a quaint cliché, the phrase "Reading is Fundamental" couldn't be more true.

I first realized the importance of reading in the lives of some of America's greatest leaders while I was reading the book "American Generalship: Character is Everything: The Art of Command" by Edgar J. Puryear, Jr. In the book, Puryear detailed some of the common traits of some of the great generals of American history. One thing they all had in common was the priority they placed on reading professionally AND for pleasure. Reading was so important to Gen. Edward C. "Shy" Meyer, chief of staff of the US Army from 1979 to 1983, that he often got up at 3:30 or 4am just to READ for his own information. Even more shocking to me was that Gen. George C. Marshall, Army Chief of Staff during World War II, took only 19 days of leave between 1939 and 1945 but still made time to READ. Take a moment to digest that. These men were leaders of thousands of men facing life and death struggles every day and they still made time to READ. Sort of makes all my excuses about being too busy to READ sound really stupid. These men placed such a high value on reading that they made time for it even in the face of what had to be overwhelming demands on their time. After learning this I set a goal for myself to read a book a month. While not at the level of some of those I read about in Puryear's book, it was a huge jump for a guy who probably hadn't read more than 1 book in 12 years. And the truth is, it got good to me. What did I read? I read a little bit of everything which I think is important was well. I read biographies, histories and Christian fiction. Since that time I will confess that my reading habits have changed slightly. The predominant amount of my reading is comic books and the bible. (I'll wait while you stop laughing.) I have majored in these two areas because one thing I love to READ about is heroes and there's no greater hero story every written than that of the bible. And because I want to be a hero to my wife, my kids, my friends and my church, I enjoy reading comic books because they embody the ideals of what I want to be. After all, I wouldn't have known that "with great power comes great responsibility" if I hadn't read Spider-Man comics. Yeah, it might seem childish but just like every great answer doesn't come from where I stand, every great answer to life's most pressing issues doesn't come from "War and Peace" either.

The bottom line is that leaders need to READ. Since we can't make all the mistakes ourselves, it's probably better to read and learn from what others have done and been through...even others like Superman, Captain America and Abraham. Make time to READ what interests you. READ what you enjoy because it will have a greater impact on your life. READ for education and entertainment. READ to expand your mind, your borders and your vocabulary. Just READ. And just maybe one day, because you've chosen to READ in order to PREPARE yourself to lead, someone will READ about you.

If we could give every individual the right amount of nourishment and exercise, not too little and not too much, we would have found the safest way to health.
-- Hippocrates

This is the "Do as I say, not as I do" portion of the book. That's not necessarily true because I'm practicing leadership like everyone else and I don't always get all of these things right all of the time. However, I'm not so naïve to know that my failure to EXERCISE regularly potentially limited my effectiveness as a leader. I have to include a disclaimer to make sure everyone is clear that I'm not trying to say that successful leaders are the ones with six-pack abs, 30-inch waists and several 26.2 stickers on the back of their cars. You don't have to be a gym rat to be a successful leader but you do need to include regular EXERCISE as part of your lifestyle to ensure your body is ready for the rigors of leadership. No leader can be effective if his or her body falls apart. While jobs have set hours of operation, leadership does not. Successful leadership is a 24/7 responsibility that requires a person to function effectively whenever duty calls. Then again, maybe it's just me. Some of my more challenging leadership opportunities came after duty hours when I thought work was done for the day. But there is my point. Work was done. Leadership was not. Because leadership can be a draining experience, EXERCISE becomes even more important to ensure the leader is prepared for those times of stress and struggle.

Perhaps the best example I can give is how my father ran basketball practice when I was a kid. We NEVER shot free throws at the beginning of practice. We would run laps, sprints and suicides, followed by drills and then play half court and then play full court. When that whistle would blow and my dad would call us over, we were beat. Many times I wanted to just fall where I was and stay there until practice the next day. It was at that point that my dad would direct us to the free throw line and challenge us to make our free throws or run sprints for every miss. Yes, this was cruel and unusual punishment but it forced us to focus on the task at hand despite how tired we were. What we didn't realize was all that EXERCISE wasn't preparing us for the end of practice. All that EXERCISE was preparing us for game time. My dad was teaching was that our bodies needed to be ready for the tougher moments because those moments were the most critical. Similarly, for the leader, it's easy to get work done at 10am because it's the first part of the day and things are good. But how about 12 hours later when decisions need to be made and the task needs to be completed? We might be OK with one 12-hour day every two weeks or so but when those long, hard days are strung together, how we prepared our bodies through EXERCISE during the slow times will determine how productive we will be.

Just as I don't care what you read, I don't believe it matters what you do in regards to EXERCISE. The point is to make it a lifestyle habit to do something to get the blood pumping and the body moving. I'm a firm believer that all EXERCISE programs work…as long as you do them. Yoga is great. Workout videos are great. Weight training and running are great. Walking is great. Just pick something that works for you and be consistent at it. As much as I hate running, and I REALLY hate running, I have to confess that I was at my best as a pastor and Air Force officer when I made a point to run at least three times a week. On those long days, and there were many, I was better able to focus on the task at hand in large part because my body had been prepared for the additional activity because those moments were not the first time my heart had been racing that week. The EXERCISE, while painful at the moment, was profitable in the end. Make time to strengthen your body through EXERCISE because you don't know when you'll be needed to hit those clutch free throws.

Taking a 3-D Look at Yourself

1. What are the priorities of your life? Don't just rattle them off, take time and list them. Once you have that list, ask those close to you if that list accurately reflects the life they see you living. What does your calendar say about that list? What does your checkbook say about that list?

2. What changes do you need to make in your life so you can better PREPARE yourself to REST, EAT, PRAY, READ and EXERCISE? Choose one of the five listed to focus on for the next 30 days and see if anything changes in your life and ability to lead.

Chapter 5: So Now What?

The call for leaders is just as loud now as it ever has been. In 2016, America experienced the most "intriguing" presidential campaign on record in search of the next "Leader of the Free World." Questions of the ability of each candidate to handle the pressures of the position were debated over and over again as those on each side attacked everything about the candidates from positions on issues to temperament. I didn't know who the best choice to lead America was but from my limited point of view, I only had three questions for each candidate:

1. Will you CARE about the Team? In your role as leader, can the people count on you to COVER, AFFIRM, RESPECT and EMPOWER them? The right leader needs to CARE because the leader must impact the team to a greater degree and grow those team members into being leaders in their own right.

2. Will you DARE the Task? In your role as leader, can the people count on you to DECIDE, ACT, RECOVER and ENERGIZE. The right leader will DARE because we do not want to just complete tasks, but complete those tasks well.

3. Will you PREPARE Yourself? In your roles as leader, can the people count on you to PRIORITIZE, REST, EAT, PRAY, ASK, READ and EXERCISE. The right leader will PREPARE because the leader needs to be around and be productive for the long haul.

Before you think I'm getting political, these questions aren't just for presidential candidates. These questions are for anyone in a leadership position. And here's a clue, we are all in leadership positions. I said it earlier but it bears repeating...Leadership is about influence. Leadership is not about position but about those who choose to follow you. While you may not have the big office or your name on the door, someone is following your lead. They are watching you to determine how to respond and where to go next. They need you to lead. A few years ago, former NBA superstar Charles Barkley made the statement that he is not a role model. While being a role model is an incredible responsibility and many would love to shirk that mantle like Mr. Barkley did, we don't get to choose if we're role models or not. People choose their role models. In the same respect, people choose their leaders. Therefore, the question really isn't, "are you a leader?" The question is, "Will you be a successful leader?"

As the pastor of St Mary AME Church in Shreveport, LA, I spend my Sundays pontificating to people the things I believe God would have them to know. I don't do this because I like to hear myself talk or because I want to entertain them. The ultimate goal of every sermon is that those who hear will apply what they've heard. Pastor Rick Warren calls it "Preaching for response." It's the thought that if the lesson isn't applied, it's wasted. Well, as I come to the close of this "sermon," my prayer is that something you have read in these pages will be applicable to your life and will make you a better leader. Whether you are leading a team of two or 200 or just yourself, the world is calling for you to lead better. Better in how you CARE, DARE and PREPARE. Better in how you manage the team, the task and yourself. Better in recognizing you haven't arrived yet and continually striving to improve in every situation you face. If you feel like you haven't been a good leader in the past, then you read this book at the exact right time in your leadership career. Show your leadership growth and RECOVER. Feel like you've been too scared to move out on the decisions you've made? Then show yourself as a better leader and ACT. Think you've let your people down? Then do better tomorrow by providing them the

COVER they need and show them the RESPECT they long for. Feeling worn down? Then be a better leader by taking time to EAT and REST. Becoming a Three-Dimensional Leader isn't about "can do." We all "can" become better. Becoming a Three-Dimensional Leader is about "want to." If you want to be a better leader, you can be by applying the lessons learned here on not just a daily basis, but on a moment-by-moment basis in every leadership situation.

My last analogy will be this one…picture yourself trying to walk up a down escalator. At the top of the escalator is becoming the leader you've always wanted to be. There is no question that you can make it to the top. The only question is, "Do you want to?" Just nodding your head isn't enough. You've got to ACT. You've got to continually step up that escalator while it is coming down at you if you want to get to the top. There are no breaks. There are no days off. The only way to achieve the goal is to continually march up those steps to being a better leader. You have to keep moving because if you don't, you won't just stay still, you will move backwards and lose ground. Therefore, I triple-dog dare you to put this book down and DARE every task that comes your way. I triple-dog dare you to look at every team member and CARE for them wholeheartedly. I triple-dog dare you to make time to PREPARE yourself. The world is hungry for some Three-Dimensional leaders and this is your season to step into that leadership void and guide yourself, your team, your company and your country into new levels of greatness. There's no question it can be done. But I ask again, do you want it?

www.ingramcontent.com/pod-product-compliance
Lightning Source LLC
Chambersburg PA
CBHW071515210326
41597CB00018B/2770